Six STEPS to Financial Fitness
Managing your money *AND* your financial advisors

Tony Bland

Infinite Possibilities Publishing Group, Inc.
Florida

This book is available at special quantity discounts for bulk purchases, sales promotions, premiums, fundraising, or educational use.

For details, write:
Special Markets, IP Publishing Group
P.O. Box 150823
Altamonte Springs, Florida 32715-0823
e-mail: info@ippublishingonline.com

IP Books
Published by Infinite Possibilities Publishing Group, Inc.
P.O. Box 150823
Altamonte Springs, Florida 32715-0823
email: info@ippublishingonline.com
Website: www.ippublishingonline.com

Copyright © 2003 by Tony Bland

All rights reserved. No part of this publication may be produced, stored in a retrieval system or transmitted in any form or by any means electronic, mechanical, photocopying, recording or otherwise, without the prior written permission of the publisher or except in the case of brief quotations embodied in critical articles and reviews.

Cover Photo by:
Riku/Anna Photography

Cover Design and text layout by:
Designs By Rachelle, Rachelle Harris
www.designsbyrachelle.com

Library of Congress Control Number: 2003115514

ISBN: 0-9729912-2-0

Printed in the United States of America

10 9 8 7 6 5 4 3 2 1

For Marina, Ashby, and Tony Jr.,
With all my love

Consumers are voiceless, so do it yourself.
-Tony Bland

Acknowledgments

I humbly acknowledge the efforts of the many friends and family who took the time to review and comment on the early versions of the manuscript. I especially appreciate the comments and encouragement of Ethel, Hank, Jonathan, and Patrick.

I also want to thank Jackie Jones for helping me find my writing voice, educating me about the book business, and for providing many of the personal testimonies for the book.

Thanks to Steve Klodt for his copyediting, Scott Miller for his estate planning expertise, Shelley Parris for her publishing help, and all the others who tirelessly reread the manuscript until perfection was achieved.

To my colleagues in the financial services business, I am hopeful that you capture the simple essence of this book and translate it to the benefit of your clients.

To the consumer, I write and speak for your benefit and your benefit alone. And, to my wife and children, thanks most of all for your patience, love and support.

Table of Contents

Introduction   7

Step 1. Set Goals and Strategies (Setting Up Your Game Plan)   10
     Goal Setting Techniques
     Strategy Setting Examples

Step 2. Create Cash Surplus (Creating Extra Money to Save)   21
     Lifestyle, Debt and Expense Control
     Cash Flow Worksheet
     Net Worth Worksheet

Step 3. Manage Cash Surplus and Pick Good Investments (Now That You Have the Money, What Do You Do with It?)   37
     Organize Your Financial Plan
     What Are Your Investment Choices?

Step 4. Pick Good Advisors (Need Help)   48
     Know Your Advisor's Motivation
     Interview Topics

Step 5. Leave a Legacy (Keep It in the Family)   56
     The Estate Plan
     Five Basic Documents

Step 6. Increase Your Financial Knowledge (Educate Yourself)   60
     What You Need to Know
     Information Sources
     Daily Learning

Special Section- Financial Makeovers (Need a Quick Fix)   66
     Financial Makeover #1
     Financial Makeover #2

Appendix - Estate Planning Documents   73

Epilogue   108

Further Reading   110

INTRODUCTION

At a young age, I learned that a little can be made into a lot. My mother raised my sisters and me on a factory worker's salary. She was good at managing her money, and over time saved enough to purchase the home that she still lives in today, more than thirty years later. Now a retiree, she has enough money to live comfortably and without financial constraints. Her experience, along with my personal experience as a registered investment advisor, manager of financial advisors, and private banker (where I was responsible for more than $200 million of wealthy individuals' money), taught me that wealthy consumers are not much different than my mom. The best money managers are disciplined, have a plan, and make the most out of a little. Both need help and guidance to make informed decisions. Even though she is smart (she was the valedictorian of her high school), my mom was at a clear disadvantage when working with financial advisors and financial products. Most consumers are in the same position—too trusting of large brokerages, banks, insurance companies, and their representatives.

To get the most from your banking, investment, and insurance relationships, you need to have a well-thought-out plan for financial success. You need to have a blueprint. When building your dream home, you rely on a blueprint to guide the contractors working on the home. Similarly, when building a financial future you should rely on a financial blueprint to guide your financial advisors. *Six Steps to Financial Fitness* gives you the blueprint.

You also need to understand the motivation of the various advisors: bankers, stockbrokers, insurance agents, trust officers, and financial advisors. These advisors have the job of guiding you through the maze of products and services. Their motivation is in direct competition with your motivation. While you are looking for objective, honest advice, they are looking for a paycheck. Their paycheck comes when you say yes to one of their proposals. Your blueprint allows you to drive the process and minimizes the negative impact of an advisor's selfish motivation.

The financial services industry is complicated to navigate and has many conflicts of interest; therefore, consumers suffer. My objective in writing this book is to provide you an easy-to-use blueprint for becoming financially fit. I want you in control, leading your family to financial fitness without the stress and anxiety often associated with financial matters.

Six Steps to Financial Fitness is designed to be a do-it-yourself guide to financial success. In *Six Steps to Financial Fitness* you will learn the six simple steps to financial fitness, receive a realistic blueprint to follow, and be provided examples to apply to your life. You will learn to pick good investments and great financial advisors. To pull it all together, you will get to view two financial makeovers that incorporate the topics discussed throughout the book. You will also receive an estate planning questionnaire to review and complete to assist you in setting up your own estate plan. My goal is to give you the tools and insight you need to blueprint your way to becoming financially fit!

STEP 1

SET GOALS AND STRATEGIES
- Setting Up Your Game Plan -

Your goals are the financial objectives you choose and your strategies are the ways that you will achieve your objectives. Start by creating your financial goals and strategies in the following six categories: (1) lifestyle, (2) emergency, (3) accumulation, (4) education, (5) retirement, and (6) legacy. Provided at the end of this chapter are blank sheets for you to document your goals and strategies using the following examples as a guide. These examples provide a format for writing your own goals and strategies. Substitute your own goals and strategies for those in the examples. You may delete words or numbers and replace them with your own or you may rewrite the examples altogether.

Lifestyle Goal

My current lifestyle goal is the financial commitment necessary to meet day-to-day living expenses and provide for future saving and investment. For example, my goal is to keep my monthly living expenses in the $3,000-to-$3,500-per-month range for the next three years, while generating approximately $1,000 cash surplus for my other five financial goals. I will live a moderate lifestyle and purchase products and services that fit within that lifestyle. For example, I will vacation in Embassy Suites hotels, not Ritz Carltons (more expensive) or Days Inns (less expensive). I will eat out at Red Lobster, not Ruth's Chris Steak House (more expensive) or McDonald's (less expensive). I will drive Chevys, not BMWs (more expensive) or Hyundai (less expensive). I will not waste money on non-appreciating items, such as cigarettes, alcoholic beverages, expensive clothing, fancy electronics or expensive foods.

Create a list of each expense in your life and build your overall lifestyle goal and strategy around it.

In addition, you may pledge something like this: For preventative reasons, I will exercise regularly and have semiannual medical, dental, and vision checkups. I will not allow physical neglect or financial waste to keep me from my goals. I will keep consumer debt (credit cards) to a minimum and maintain one credit card for convenience only. If I use a credit card, then I will pay off the balance when I receive the next statement. My approach to using credit is to gain a return greater than the cost of the credit. I will live at least 25 percent below my means.

Emergency Goal

My emergency goal is to create a liquid nest egg in case of an unexpected problem, such as loss of my job, a major automobile repair, or helping out my parents. This goal is equal to six months of my income. For example, my goal is to save $10,800 in a low-risk, tax-free money market account during the next year and a half. I will save $10,800 by putting $600 per month into my money market account for eighteen months. Once I reach this goal I shall maintain it or, if I am forced to use parts of it for an emergency, replenish it. As my income rises I shall increase my emergency fund. This fund will be used to cover bills if I suddenly become unemployed, or for repair of major household appliances, or my car. This is not a loan fund for relatives seeking to borrow money or a "slush fund" for impulsive spending. This is my emergency safety net.

Accumulation Goal

My accumulation goal is a longer-term goal to achieve a specific objective or make a specific purchase (a big-ticket item). For example, my accumulation goal is to save $200 per month for the next two years to accumulate $4,800 for a 5-percent down payment on the purchase of a rental property. I will also save $100 per month for the next three years to take a trip to Europe or Africa. My goal is to save $3,600 for this trip. I will save this money in a low-risk money market account or in certificates of deposit, whichever is paying the higher interest rate. If possible, I will find a bank or credit union willing to give me CDs without a penalty for early withdrawal.

Education Goal

My education goal is to save for my children's college education at one of the better public universities in the state of my residence. For example, my education goal is to invest $175 per month in a prepaid college program for my three children. The eldest child will be allocated ninety dollars, the middle child fifty-five dollars, and the youngest thirty dollars per month to pay for their tuition, room, and board, based on the state's prepaid college program. I will continue these payments until each child's education cost is fully guaranteed and paid for. My personal educational goal is to attend a graduate school. It will cost approximately $10,000 to attend a local university. My job will pay for $5,000 of the school expenses through our employee benefit program. I have applied for and received a scholarship from the university for $1,400. For my shortfall of $3,600, I will save $300 per month over the next year to have the entire $10,000 available for next year's master's program. I will not finance this educational goal with debt.

Retirement Goal

My retirement goal is to pay for my living expenses upon my retirement from full-time work at about age 65. To meet this goal, I have calculated that I need to accumulate approximately $400,000 in cash. I will contribute $8,500 per year into my 401(k) plan and invest that money in moderate to conservative investments. My plan is to earn an average of 6 percent each year (over the next twenty-eight years) without a high potential for loss of principal. I will also supplement my 401(k) with a ROTH IRA contribution of $3,000 per year. I anticipate that $300,000 of the $400,000 goal will be from my 401(k) and will require taxable distributions. The $100,000 will be from my tax-free Roth IRA. This amount combined with my social security of approximately $1,200 per month will be sufficient for me to comfortably live out my life. I will have my current home paid in full (twenty-eight years left on the mortgage), and I will purchase a new automobile immediately prior to my retirement. During retirement, I will live a more conservative lifestyle than the lifestyle I lived before I retired.

Legacy Goal

My legacy goal is to insure my family and property against any casualty that may impact our lifestyle, health, or finances. In addition, my goal is to ensure that my family's financial goals can be met if I die prematurely or my wife dies. For example, I will maintain property and health insurance premiums that provide for the lowest deductibles available. My life insurance policies will be twenty-year term policies with $250,000 face values. I will review my coverage amounts annually to ensure that survivor cash and income needs can be covered by the face amount of the policies. Furthermore, upon reaching the age of sixty, I shall purchase long-term care insurance to protect my estate against potential loss due to payment of health facility costs. I will have my will and trust documents completed by my fortieth birthday. After we have died, my spouse and I want to leave a minimum of $250,000 to our heirs.

In summary, you should start writing down your initial goals and strategies in a general way. Go back and revisit them to add detail, as needed. Goals do not have to be complicated, but should be financially specific. The more detailed the better, but you do not want to get bogged down in the detail either. The keys are to write down your goals, use specific numbers, and revisit your strategies often. Any goals that require investment in stocks, mutual funds, or the like should be reviewed weekly at a minimum. Do not "go to sleep" on those investments. Eventually, you'll be on automatic pilot and achieving your goals without giving them a second thought.

Lifestyle

Emergency

Accumulation

Education

Retirement

Legacy

STEP 2

CREATE CASH SURPLUS
- Creating Extra Money to Save -

Cash surplus results from how well you manage your lifestyle. Your lifestyle is your everyday financial behavior. Control your lifestyle spending to maximize the surplus cash you have to invest for your future. The surplus formula is income (take-home pay) minus lifestyle equals surplus (I-L=S). To create a future you can count on, simply increase your employment income and consistently live below your means.

You may not rely on a written budget to track expenses (it is too rigid for many people) and that is okay. It may be more natural for you to create cash surplus without using a written budget. You may simply change your daily lifestyle to spend less, knowing your surplus will grow.

For those who need to track their expenses with a written budget, continue to do so, but supplement your tracking with a sense of your lifestyle. Paying attention to your lifestyle may encourage you to catch those "little" items that sometimes do not make it into your budget.

Use the Lifestyle Budget Worksheet (Exhibit 1) to plan your spending and create your cash surplus. Once you have completed your worksheet, compare it to your actual spending patterns to find areas of waste and inefficiencies. Key in on your use of credit and limit the payment of compound interest by paying off all credit-related bills as quickly as possible. Consider your residence an asset that affords you a mortgage interest deduction on your tax return. It is financially important to purchase your house in a neighborhood whose homes will increase in value.

Assuming your lifestyle choice is to live below your means, you should review the spending categories in your lifestyle budget and reduce the dollar amounts of each. You should also change any behavior that causes you to exceed your budget.

To use the Lifestyle Budget Worksheet, just fill in the blanks with information from your checkbook or from your computerized budget. Don't forget to include your cash purchases. Feel free to customize the Lifestyle Budget Worksheet to your specific needs.

Each day, be sure to minimize or eliminate debt, eliminate unnecessary spending, and manage all expenses to maximize your cash surplus. This simple focus leaves you cash to save and manage. Each dollar lost or wasted today multiplies the loss for tomorrow. For example, $140 saved per month earning an 8-percent return over a thirty-year period grows to more than $150,000.

The ultimate measure of your success in using your surplus is your net worth. Net worth equals your assets minus your liabilities (N=A-L). Your scorecard for how well you have used your cash surplus is your Net Worth Worksheet. Exhibit 2 shows a blank Net Worth Worksheet. Use it to create your own worksheet. The higher your net worth, the better you are using your cash surplus. You should continually work to increase your net worth.

Exhibit 1

Lifestyle Budget Worksheet

Income

    Net Income $_____

Expenses

Housing *(rent, mortgage, etc.)*	$_____
Automobile/Transportation	$_____
Utilities *(telephone, electric, water, gas, etc.)*	$_____
Food and Clothing	$_____
Debt Payments	$_____
Medical	$_____
Insurance	$_____
Family/Day Care	$_____
Education	$_____
Gifts	$_____
Entertainment	$_____
_____	$_____
_____	$_____
_____	$_____

Total Expenses $_____

Cash Surplus (Income minus Expenses) $_____

Exhibit 2

Net Worth Worksheet

Description	Assets	Liabilities
Checking Accounts	$_____	$_____
Savings Accounts	$_____	$_____
Money Market Accounts	$_____	$_____
CDs	$_____	$_____
Mutual Funds	$_____	$_____
Stocks and Bonds	$_____	$_____
Rental Property	$_____	$_____
Personal Residence	$_____	$_____
Business Interests	$_____	$_____
Automobiles	$_____	$_____
Personal Property	$_____	$_____
Retirement Accounts		
401(k)/403(b)	$_____	$_____
IRA	$_____	$_____
Life Insurance Cash Value	$_____	$_____
Credit Card/Loans	$_____	$_____

Other Assets or Liabilities

_____	$_____	$_____
_____	$_____	$_____
_____	$_____	$_____

Total Assets and Liabilities $_____ $_____

Net Worth *(Assets minus Liabilities)* $_____

Tips to build cash surplus

- **Minimize fixed expenses**
  - housing, automobile, cable television, etc.
- **Control variable expenses**
  - credit cards, telephone, shopping, etc.
- **Increase income**
  - second job, promotion, raise, etc.
- **Live below your means – don't try to keep up with the Joneses**
- **Realize... it's not what you make, it's what you spend**

www.finfitco.com

Financial Fitness Company of America

More tips for building surplus.....

- **Organize paperwork**
  - investments
  - bills
- **Manage checkbook**
  - use check register
  - reconcile with statement
- **Cut up credit cards**
- **Use debit cards**
- **Lower your clothing bill**
- **Eat at home**

- **Keep autos for 10 years**
  - buy used
- **Buy the smaller home**
- **Stop buying**
  - fast foods and soft drinks
  - liquor and cigarettes
- **Bag your lunch**
- **Check your utilities**
- **If it's not broken, don't fix it**

www.finfitco.com

Financial Fitness Company of America

STEP 2 - CREATE CASH SURPLUS

More tips for building surplus.....

- **Make investments that pay you income**
- **Purchase profitable rental property**
- **Make tax-free investments**
- **Set up a small business**
- **Work two or more jobs at the same time**
- **Tax plan**
- **Shop for the highest-yielding investments**

www.finfitco.com

Financial Fitness Company of America

Motivational Testimonials

Building cash surplus takes discipline. Many times the difference between success and failure is your ability to say "no" to yourself and to others. Following are real life testimonials of people who found ways to increase their cash surplus, before and during retirement.

Testimonial #1: A Little Means a Lot

When I was in college I had an aunt who traveled extensively, usually taking cruises. My aunt had a decent job, but her bank account wasn't overflowing with money. She had a nice home, decorated with things she had bought over the years and taken good care of. One day, while I was visiting my aunt, her boyfriend, a postal worker, came by her house to visit. Before he sat down, he took all the loose change out of his pocket and put it in a huge jar tucked away in a corner of the living room. He explained that each day he and my aunt put their loose change in the jar. "That's how we save for our vacations," he said. "You'd be surprised how that adds up."

I remembered that story and years later, when my money was tight, but I wasn't willing to give up on vacations, I started to do the same. From one year to the next I was able to save up to a couple hundred dollars that I could spend without taking money away from another budget item or my regular savings. I generally went to places close to home and drove, saving even more money, often staying with friends or relatives. Having some money to burn made the vacations even nicer.

Recently, although I can more easily budget for vacations, I have once again begun putting my loose change in a jar, just to see how much accumulates over several months.

Testimonial #2: A Savings Trick

I was notoriously bad at saving money, so I developed a couple of ways of "tricking" myself into saving.

I would open a savings account at a small bank that didn't have branches all over the country. I had a portion of my check direct deposited or would make mail deposits each payday, but I would not get an ATM card. That way, if I wanted to withdraw money, I'd have to make a special trip. It gave me time to decide whether I really needed the money or just wanted to blow a little on something frivolous. If the withdrawal was worth the time and energy to get it, then the purchase really needed to be worthy. Having money out of reach helped me save more than $1,000 the first year. Not bad for someone who, at the time, made only about $15,000 a year.

The next trick would be to pretend that part of my check didn't exist. Say, for example, that your take-home pay for a week is

$323.59. Pretend that the $23.59 isn't there, and base your budgeting on $300 a week. In six weeks, you have $141.54 surplus. Transfer it into your savings account and forget about it. Once you accumulate a substantial amount in savings, you can determine whether to contribute to your ROTH IRA or put it in a money market account or some account that earns you better interest than a regular savings account. I still budget that way.

Testimonial #3: Maintain or Downsize Your Lifestyle

My dad told me once that I would get to a point where I could live comfortably on the money I made. "Once you get there, try to stay there. Every time you get a raise, don't try to live up to the new money," he said. In other words, if your take-home pay goes up fifty dollars a payday, don't think about what you now can afford with the extra money. Don't start buying filet mignon, when you've been buying ground beef. Bank that extra fifty dollars. Don't start getting your nails done every week instead of doing them yourself. Just keep living at the same level. It helps build that savings cushion you need. If, for some reason, you have to take a pay cut or get laid off, you've put money away to fall back on instead of having to worry about how you're going to pay your bills when you've just added a new bill to your lifestyle.

If you're close to retirement, it's wise to figure out what your monthly pension and social security payment will be and start figuring out how to live on that income. My dad found out what his monthly payment would be and paid his bills and cut back on some spending based on what he had to work with. By the time he retired, he was able to live off his pension without taking on a part-time job.

Things are a bit different, though, for baby boomers.

Many boomer retirees will still be paying house notes, car notes, and trying to maintain the same lifestyle they had while they were working. Those are the folks running the jitney service at the grocery store or working part-time at the local Wal-Mart or Home

Depot. They'll tell you they like to keep busy, but usually it's because their pensions do not cover all the bills. It is a good idea to make the downsizing adjustments in your lifestyle prior to retirement. Selling the bigger house and buying a smaller house will cut all your living expenses and put money in your pocket from the sale (if you bought the original house in an appreciating neighborhood). Getting a smaller car will save gas and other expenses while also making it easier to drive and park. Try to find entertainment and activities that aren't costly to seniors; this will decrease those extra little expenses that can add up over time.

Testimonial #4: It's Okay to Say "No"

My downfall was that whenever I would get ahead, develop a little cushion, I'd loan money to friends or family members in need, knowing that I probably would never see that money again. I understand what it's like to be broke, dodging bill collectors, wondering if I will ever be able to breathe easy again. I wanted to be able to help others get on their feet.

Your goal is to have the equivalent of at least six months' pay in the bank in case of emergency. You can't loan it and have it, too. So, even when your bank account starts looking pretty good, it's okay to tell someone, as my mom says, "I don't have any money to loan." Notice that she didn't say she did not have any money. She said she had none to loan. There's enough money in the bank to address her needs and the majority of her wants. If she starts loaning money to people, however, that could disappear. Once the word is out that you're willing to help someone financially, you'll have friends and family at your door hitting you up for small loans of fifty dollars here, a few hundred dollars there. Soon, you're owed substantial amounts of money that you can't collect because you loaned it on the honor system. Most likely, you don't make anyone sign an agreement to repay at a certain rate of interest. Because you are mom, dad, grandma, auntie, uncle, older brother, rich sister, best friend, etc., your loved ones don't have the same sense of urgency about repaying you as they do MasterCard or Visa accounts.

If you confront the borrowers, they're going to feel angry and embarrassed and try to make you feel guilty for asking for repayment. They might reply, "I said I would pay you when I get it." "My check hasn't come in yet." "Quit hounding me, will you? You know I'm good for it." You may have heard these excuses before. As I tell my son, "If you can get money to pay me back, you don't need to borrow because you can figure out how to get the money and pay the bill."

He and I have an agreement now. He will ask me for what he wants. If I have it to spare, I'll give it to him. If I don't, I won't. I don't take credit card advances to send him money via Western Union and I tune out the hard-luck stories.

Saying no is difficult the first time. After you do it successfully, it gets easier. Now my son doesn't bother to ask. We get along beautifully.

Testimonial #5: Cash Only

For years I struggled to get a handle on my spending. I would go to the mall or supermarket and shop till I dropped. If I was hungry I spent more at the grocery store, usually on impulse items, such as cakes, cookies, candy and potato chips, that weren't good for me. If I was depressed I spent more at the mall—a new dress for an event that would never happen or a new pair of shoes to make me feel good. Either way I would typically spend more than I had in my pocket and use my credit card or debit card to pay the bill.

After years of this buying pattern I realized that my saving problem was due to my inability to control my spending. So I came up with a plan.

Once I determined my budget for the week, I would schedule myself to go shopping (no longer impulse). I would go to the bank and withdraw the exact cash amount I budgeted for that shopping appointment. So, if my budget was fifty dollars for food that week, I would pull out fifty dollars cash and go to the supermarket. I would shop, get to the register and if I had more than that amount in groceries, something would not be bought. I would do the same thing at the mall, and eventually with other activities, such as eating out or going to the movies.

It changed my life! I don't carry credit cards and never use my debit card. I do it the old fashioned way, cash. This forces me to follow my budget and prioritize my spending. It is not easy, but I now spend less money and feel better about myself. I also have more money to put into my savings and investment plans.

The following blank pages have been provided for you to document your Lifestyle Budget Worksheet and Net Worth Budget Worksheet using Exhibits 1 and 2 as your guide.

Lifestyle Budget Worksheet

Lifestyle Budget Worksheet

Net Worth Budget Worksheet

Net Worth Budget Worksheet

STEP 3

MANAGE CASH SURPLUS AND PICK GOOD INVESTMENTS
- Now That You Have the Money, What Do You Do with It? -

Once you have cash surplus remaining from your lifestyle, allocate the surplus to your other five goals. For example, if you have $500 in surplus, you may put $50 into emergency, $100 into accumulation, $50 into education, $200 into retirement, and $100 into legacy. Divide the cash based on the strategy you have created for each of the five goals and use the Financial Fitness Funding Model in Exhibit 3 to guide your choice of products for your five goals. Exhibit 3 shows how your plan may look using the financial products you can choose to match to your goals. Keep in mind that real estate owned for investment purposes can help you meet many of your goals. Real estate can be bought and sold, borrowed against, or used as a cash generator for your short- and long-term needs.

Step 3 – Manage Cash Surplus and Pick Good Investments

Exhibit 3

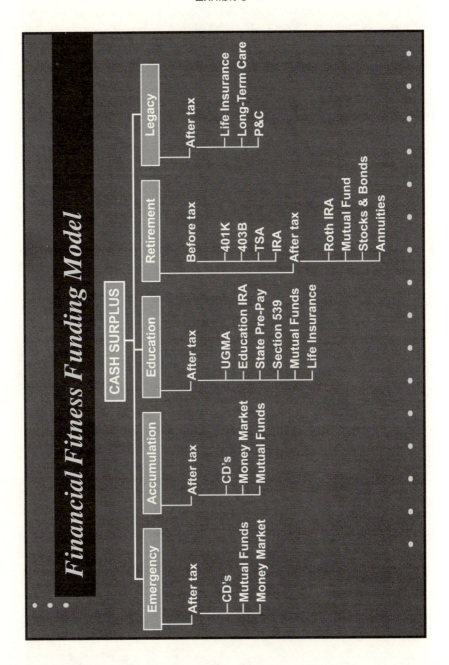

Your **Emergency Goal** is generally a short-term goal. If you have an emergency, you want to have access to your money without the risk of principal loss or fees. Therefore, you want to put that money in liquid investments, such as money market products or certificates of deposit (CD). You want to purchase a CD from a bank that will not charge you a fee for cashing out before the CD matures. Shop for the best rates.

Your **Accumulation Goal** is longer-term and generally you have more time to keep that money in its investment product; therefore, you may use money market products, CDs, mutual funds, or individual bonds. Your highest risk is with mutual funds. Mutual fund investing with a specific exit strategy requires you to pay close attention to fees and volatility of the fund. If you choose to pick a fund, pick one with minimal risk to principal and without liquidation fees. No-load mutual funds generally have no up-front charges and low liquidation fees.

Your **Education Goal** is generally longer-term and theoretically you can take more risk and invest in equity mutual funds and individual stocks to meet this goal. If you think that saving for a child's college education is something that should not be put at risk, however, you can guarantee your child's education by enrolling in one of the many state-run pre-pay programs. Otherwise, there are many other ways to save for college if you have time on your side and do not mind taking risk. Section 529 plans offer great tax breaks for the wealthy and are very popular with investors. The Uniform Gift To Minors Act allows you to put away money for a child and let it grow at the child's lower tax rate. Upon age of majority (18 or 21 in most states), however, children can legally take the money and do with it what they wish, college or not. Many parents do not like this feature. If you do not have time on your side or do not like risk, then you will want to be very conservative in your choices. Don't forget, this goal is to pay for a child's education first, not get a tax break or play in the market. Regardless of your feelings about risk, you should always be cautious in researching and selecting your investment products.

Your **Retirement Goal** is usually long-term and lends itself to investments in either a pre-tax employer sponsored plan, such as a 401(k), or an after-tax plan, such as a Roth IRA. A combination of the two may be a good long-term strategy, given their contrasting tax benefits at distribution. The strategy is driven by the unpredictability of future income tax rates. Because you do not know what tax rates will be when you retire and distributions from your 401(k) are taxable, it is smart to have a source of tax-free money. At retirement, distributions from your Roth IRA are tax-free. So, the distribution strategy is: if tax rates are high you will take the money from your Roth (it's tax-free), and if tax rates are low you will take the money from your 401(k) (it's taxable). This strategy gives you the flexibility to take advantage of the tax rate regardless the rate during your retirement.

Be sure to look at all the options for saving long-term, or if you are near retirement, the shorter-term. Make sure that your choice matches your time frame for needing the money and has a favorable fee structure. In determining what to invest your retirement money in, the terms asset allocation and diversification often come up as the way to decrease risk in your portfolio of investments. Usually, a financial advisor will have you complete a risk questionnaire that leads to a pie chart of various mutual fund asset classes. Those classes generally include, large-cap growth, large-cap value, mid-cap growth, mid-cap value, small-cap growth, small-cap value, international, bonds, and so on. Your pie chart will tell you what percentage to place in each category to achieve your desired return rate (say 12 percent) over your time horizon for retirement. Your advisor will allocate your money according to the percentages in the pie chart in mutual funds that match the asset classes described and will assure you your money will grow forever (yeah, right!). You will occasionally rebalance your portfolio (sell your winners and invest more in your losers) to keep up the percentages.

Sell winners and buy losers? This system of asset allocation and rebalancing is flawed and is a function of the industry trying to service too many customers. This questionnaire, allocation, rebalancing process is a cookie cutter way of working with clients who the industry generally feels are not individually profitable. If you are already involved in this process with a financial advisor, use their recommendations as a starting point for discussion only.

Because your retirement is important, you have to "lock into" your feelings about money and make investment decisions that may be more conservative and less volatile than your advisor may like. Your advisor's recommendation may be an 80/20 mix of mutual funds and fixed income (bonds) and you may feel more comfortable with a 20/80 mix of mutual funds and bonds. Do not feel apologetic for stating how you feel or for overruling your advisor's recommendation, especially if your choice is to be more conservative. Remember, it is your money, and as one of my favorite retired clients says, "It is surely good to sleep at night." This particular client is a millionaire and has always invested primarily in CDs and real estate—less volatile investments. Always remember, what you invest in is a personal choice. It may seem easier to have someone to make decisions for you, and you may be comfortable keeping your head in the sand. You have to resist these tendencies and take control. If you do not feel confident yet, it is still okay to make conservative decisions within your comfort zone, regardless what others are doing. If you are like my retired client, sometimes you will earn more than everyone else, and sometimes you will earn less. What she liked, though, is that she never lost money. Her conservative strategy made her a millionaire.

Your **Legacy Goal** is both short-term and very long-term. This goal is shorter-term while you are alive and prevents loss of your estate due to illness (long-term care insurance) or due to lack of adequate property and casualty insurance coverage. Generally though, this goal is long-term and can be met with life insurance and an estate plan. Life insurance comes in many types: whole life, term, universal, and variable universal, to name a few. Your selection should be based on how well you understand the product, its features and its benefits to you and your estate. A rule of thumb for life insurance is to purchase no more than ten times your annual income. Also, having a life insurance policy properly owned by a trust keeps life insurance proceeds out of your estate, and may save your estate from federal estate taxes. There are great sales pitches for these products, but by having a plan in mind prior to meeting with an advisor, you will go a long way toward staying within your comfort zone and still achieving your goal. You should give yourself some time to research these products prior to selecting an insurance agent and a policy for your plan. Make it your plan, not the agent's plan for you.

General estate planning concepts and checklists are included in Step 5, Leave a Legacy, and in the appendix.

Smart Investing

In deciding how to allocate your surplus, choose financial products based on how they match with your risk tolerance, investment objective and time frame for needing the money. Good investment choices are based on your view of money and your money psychology. Ask yourself the questions: How much money did I have growing up? What is a lot of money to me? Do I need to be rich? Do I feel good putting my hard earned money at risk? These questions help you decide how much money you really need to be happy. Don't let greed become your friend.

Your advisor will attempt to document your risk tolerance with a questionnaire. Do not let your advisor drive your investment choices based on a generic risk questionnaire and a pie chart. Those tools are designed to protect the advisor from a potential lawsuit and from your potential dissatisfaction with the performance of your portfolio. The advisor's fallback position is that investment decisions were based on your answers to the questionnaire. Whatever your view, you will want to be conservative until you have educated yourself to the point where you are confident of your investment decision-making ability. In short, always stick to what you know best.

In general,

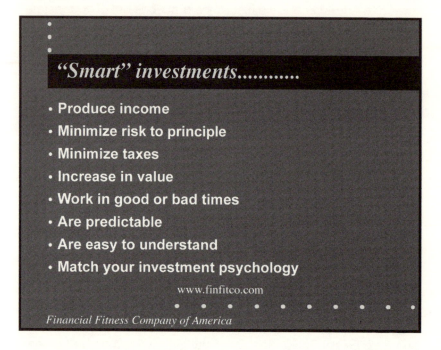

Any monies invested in the stock market should be reviewed weekly at a minimum and preferably daily. This goes for both individual stocks and mutual funds. Do not ever let your losses go above 8 percent in any of your stock or mutual fund investments. If you are like I am and dislike losing money, be aware of the moves in your portfolio and be ready to act at a moment's notice.

Advisors will tell you that you can come back from major losses in the market. Why have major losses in the first place? Advisors also will tell you to stay the course while your portfolio value is shrinking. Who wants to keep a losing strategy? Advisors tell you that if you have a long-term investment horizon, you can take more risk by investing more of your hard earned money in the stock market. I believe that if you have more time to achieve something (long-term horizon) then you can be more patient (take less risk) as you follow the path to achieving it. Do not be fooled. Advisors are financially motivated to get you to take more risk. You have to be cautious and seek all investment options prior to making your investment decisions. Do not be rushed. While you are deciding, it is okay to do nothing and let your money sit in a money market product. The bottom line question becomes: Which do you prefer, a guarantee of gain or a risk of loss? If you want a guarantee of gain, then you should invest more conservatively in bonds (held to maturity), CDs, and well-located real estate. If you are comfortable with the risk of loss, then you should invest more aggressively in stocks, mutual funds, hedge funds, and speculative real estate. For the more sophisticated investor, there are ways to hedge against losses in these more aggressive investments. But, if you are the average investor just trying to get to the end of the game (a safe retirement and a nest egg), then you may want to KISS (keep it simple stupid) and grow rich slowly and conservatively. For most people, the key to achieving wealth is increasing your income and living below your means, not the success of stock or mutual fund investments. So, make more money and invest your surplus conservatively to guarantee your retirement nest egg.

One conservative strategy is called a "bond ladder." Bonds are debt obligations issued by either a government body or a corporation looking to raise money for its operations. When you purchase a bond you are lending money to the issuer. In return, the issuer promises to pay you the face value of the bond and a periodic interest payment. It is similar to what you promise when you borrow money from a bank. You promise to pay the bank the borrowed amount and periodic interest payments. In the case of bonds, you are the bank.

A ladder is simply a layering of bonds with different maturity dates. Your money is spread over multiple periods of time. See Exhibit 4 for a visual picture of a bond ladder.

The strategy is especially good when interest rates are expected to rise. When, for example, a two-year bond matures, you take the proceeds and purchase a five-year bond. When the three-year bond matures you take the proceeds and purchase another five-year bond, and so on. This way, as the lower-rate short-term bonds mature, you use the proceeds to buy higher-rate longer-term bonds. You continue this process until rates get high enough (8 to12 percent) for you to put all your money into intermediate-term (ten- to fifteen-year) bonds. The ladder gives you short-term flexibility (you continually have money coming due), and you have the ability to take advantage of future higher rates. You also receive predictable interest payments. This money can be reinvested or used as an income source to support yourself.

For some people, holding bonds until maturity is boring low-risk investing. For the conservative investor seeking low risk and a long-term strategy, it is a great way to grow rich slowly. Keep in mind though, that as interest rates go up the value of a bond goes down. That is why in a ladder you keep bonds until they mature. If you drop the strategy and decide to sell bonds before they mature, you take the risk of not getting the face amount of the bonds, or if rates have gone down you may be able to get more than the face value. The ladder strategy keeps investing simple and doesn't require you to watch the market every minute of the day. The ladder works with city, county, state, federal, and corporate bonds. In general, corporate bonds are riskier than government bonds. All things being equal, tax-free bonds (municipals) have less risk and generally lower interest rates than corporate bonds. Pre-refunded municipal bonds are even more conservative. Pre-res, as they are called, pay a little less interest because the risk is lower than typical municipal bonds. The risk is lower with pre-res because issuers set aside a pool of money at issue to cover the bonds' payments. This product is for the most conservative bond investor. I have a client who has $9.5 million of tax-free pre-refunded municipal bonds in her portfolio. She gets tax-free income to live off ($365,000 per year) and enjoys the activity of turning over bonds as they mature. Her comment to me about the bonds is characteristic of a smart investor: "Why take risk when you don't have to?"

Exhibit 4
Bond Ladder

Total to invest is $100,000

Term	Interest rate	Amount	Quality
2005	3.25%	$25,000	AAA
2007	3.75%	$25,000	AAA
2008	4.25%	$25,000	AAA
2010	4.75%	$25,000	AAA

The average rate is 4 percent on the $100,000. Assuming a rising interest rate environment, in two years, when the 2005 matures, you take the $25,000 and purchase a 2012 bond, and so on, until rates rise high enough (8 to 12 percent) to make a longer-term commitment, say ten to fifteen years. Generally, the additional yield on bonds with maturities longer than twenty years is not worth the interest rate risk.

STEP 4

PICK GOOD ADVISORS
- Need Help -

In the 2001 Annual Securities Industry Association Investor Survey, dishonesty and poor service were the most mentioned reasons why investors may have an unfavorable impression of the securities (stock market) industry. More than 50 percent of investors view greed as a big problem for the industry.

Art Levitt, former chairman of the Securities and Exchange Commission, states in his book *Take On The Street,* "Investors today are being fed lies and distortions, are being exploited and neglected. In the wake of the last decade's rush to invest by millions of households and Wall Street's obsession with short-term performance, a culture of gamesmanship has grown among corporate management, financial analysts, brokers, and fund managers, making it hard to tell financial fantasy from reality, salesmanship from honest advice."

There is almost no way to get around working with a financial advisor. However, it is helpful if you know what you are trying to accomplish prior to hiring an advisor. So, before you select an advisor, put together your game plan based on the information presented in this book. Share your personalized financial blueprint with the selected advisor to guide the tasks you would like accomplished. The retail distribution system for financial products is set up so that, except in the case of corporations that allow consumers a direct purchase of stock, you have to use a broker, banker, or insurance agent to purchase products. To make sure the advisor you choose to work with is capable, you have to interview, interview, interview. Following is a list of interview topics to cover with your potential advisor. Provided at the end of this chapter are blank pages for you to create your own personalized list of questions from these topics. To ensure an apples-to-apples comparison, ask all advisors the same questions. I suggest interviewing at least three individuals from different companies. You can make an informed decision by comparing their answers and deciding which answers best suit you. When reviewing their answers, look for honesty, low costs, judgment, and a sincere commitment to meeting your personalized needs.

Topics to cover with your Advisor

Personal
- Family
- Education
- Experience
- Credentials/Licensing

Company
- History
- Core Competence
- Financial Stability
- Local Office Turnover
- Leadership Changes

Clients
- Number of Clients
- Mix by Investment Portfolio
- Mix by Product Types
- Mix by Asset Allocation
- Client Satisfaction Rating/References

Tools
- Financial Planning
- Asset Allocation
- Risk Assessment
- Estate Planning

Products and Costs
- Stocks and Bonds

- Mutual Funds
- Annuities
- Life Insurance
- Non-brokerage Credit
- Banking
- Trust Services
- Brokerage
- Managed Money
- Hedge Funds
- Derivatives

Philosophy
- Client-centered or Self-centered
- Proactive Communications

Process
- Multiple Steps
- Personalized Approach

People
- Teammates
- Organizational Structure

Price
- Commission
- Internal Product Costs
- Fee for Service
- Fee for Planning
- Managed Money Fee

Service
- Expectations
- Client Satisfaction Surveys

Partners
- CPA
- Attorney
- Portfolio Manager
- Fiduciary
- Banker
- Insurance Agent
- Planner
- Charitable Foundation

Once you have selected an advisor, it is time to bring him or her into your financial planning process to execute the transactions that will make your plan work. Your advisor should review your plan and suggest specific products to you for comparison and selection. The relationship with your advisor can be long-term, so be sure to regularly communicate your honest feelings and thoughts to the advisor. Also, encourage this person to reciprocate with open, honest and timely communication. You want an advisor that makes you feel like you are his or her only client. Never feel apologetic for asking your advisor about your portfolio or its performance.

In working with an advisor, one of the typical "games" you have to be aware of is the benchmark game. In the benchmark game, your advisor will attempt to convince you that you should judge your portfolio's performance by its relative performance to an established benchmark (the Standard & Poor's 500 and the Russell 2000 are common). The problem with using benchmarks is that achievement of your return goal may not require the same level of risk as the benchmark. Attempting to achieve 8 percent is not as risky as attempting to achieve 12 percent. You may also hear, "You did better than the benchmark, the S&P 500 was down 12 percent and you were down only 10 percent," the implication being that you should be happy beating the benchmark. My contention is that you should not be happy losing money and that your goal should be always to have a positive return. On the flip side, if the S&P 500 is up 20 percent, and your portfolio is up 12 percent and meeting your return goals (your goal may be to earn 8 percent per year), then you should be happy. Unless you have invested in an index fund that mirrors the benchmark, your investment will not have the same risk characteristic as the benchmark. Your investment's performance, therefore, will always be different than the benchmark, and you should question the advisor about using a benchmark to measure performance. Your portfolio's performance is an absolute, not a relative occurrence. Don't let the advisor hide behind a benchmark.

In the financial planning area, the advisor's assumptions about inflation, your age at death, and the income you need in retirement are the variables that drive the financial plan that you will receive. If the advisor is more aggressive with these assumptions, your need will be greater. A greater need translates into your need for a higher investment return to meet that need, which in turn translates into the advisor's recommendation to invest a higher percentage of your money into the stock market. I would suggest that you have your advisor present a more conservative option that assumes a lower inflation rate, a younger age of death, and a smaller income need in retirement. You can now compare the various options and can make a more informed investment decision based on your true risk tolerance and your specific goals.

Questions To Ask My Advisor

Questions To Ask My Advisor

STEP 5

LEAVE A LEGACY
- Keep It in the Family -

Five basic documents are necessary to have an estate plan. Generally, most estate plans will include the following five written documents.

1. Revocable Living Trust
2. Will
3. Power of Attorney
4. Heath Care Surrogate
5. Living Will

A trust is the written document created when you (the trustor) transfer to a trustee (a person or corporation) assets (money, real estate, stocks, mutual funds, etc.) to be held for the benefit of yourself or others (beneficiaries). If the trust is created while you are alive, it is a living trust. When you retain the right to change the trust, it is considered a revocable living trust. Trusts let you put conditions on the distribution of your assets upon your death. Used correctly, trusts also assist in the reduction of estate and gift tax, minimize the costs of probate, and may offer greater protection of your assets from creditors and lawsuits. Trusts may also be formed at your death.

Since a trust incorporates the benefits of a traditional will with greater advantages, your will is used solely to take care of assets (usually personal belongings) outside of your trust.

A power of attorney is a written document you use to give another person the power to act on your behalf. Usually, this power relates to financial and business decisions. In many states the health care surrogate and the living will have been combined into a single document called the Advanced Health Care Directives (AHCD). This document allows you to designate another person to make health care decisions, including the power to make end-of-life decisions in the case of your incapacity. You will need to hire an estate attorney to draft these documents.

In this book's appendix, you will find a blank estate-planning questionnaire and a checklist. Complete the questionnaire and provide it and the items on the checklist to your estate planning attorney at your initial meeting. The completed questionnaire will give you a head start on the process of drafting your five basic documents. The questionnaire will also challenge you to think about some things you may not have thought about. For example, if you and your spouse die simultaneously, who will care for your children? Or, if you have a child with a disability, how will the child's needs be met after you are gone? If you become incapacitated, who will make business or health-related decisions on your behalf? You will want to hire an attorney that specializes in estate planning in your state of legal residence. Attorneys will charge a fee in the neighborhood of $1,500 to $3,000 for a basic plan. If you have a substantial estate, the plan is worth the cost because you control your estate and because of the potential savings from federal estate tax on your estate and those of your heirs.

To assist with the settlement of your estate it is wise to set up a book that lists important assets, locations of important documents, keys, safe deposit boxes, business associates, doctors, financial advisors, funeral wishes, etcetera. This book will give your survivors an easier way to settle your affairs after your death.

There are additional documents and strategies that may be helpful in preserving your legacy, such as family limited partnerships, and charitable remainder trusts, to name a few. If needed, your attorney will discuss these strategies with you. If you are able, it is best to locate an attorney or financial advisor through a referral rather than through the yellow pages. Ask someone you trust and respect for a referral to an experienced estate planning attorney.

Why have an estate plan? Your estate plan is your plan (after your death) for distribution of your money, guardianship of your children, care of a disabled loved one, and contribution to your favorite charity, to name just a few of its purposes. It is your last say about your affairs. Without it, the state government will provide its plan for distribution of your money and guardianship of your children. Take time to review the checklist and the questionnaire in the appendix. This will help prepare you for your meeting with your estate planning attorney. Your attorney will let you know which combination of documents you will need to complete your personalized estate plan.

STEP 6

INCREASE YOUR FINANCIAL KNOWLEDGE
- Educate Yourself -

It is unfortunate, but you are on your own when it comes to getting financial knowledge. The 2001 Annual Securities Industry Association Investor Survey shows that 84 percent of investors feel that the securities industry should be doing more to educate the public about how to make good investments. This percentage has steadily increased, beginning in 1995 with 76 percent of investors.

Because the industry does little to educate you, it is important to become the leader of your own financial destiny. To be a good leader, you need to know something of the subject that you are called upon to lead. You probably did not receive personal finance education in high school, college, or on your job. If you have a 401(k) or other employer sponsored retirement plan, you may receive some education from the investment company that supplied your company with the 401(k) plan. This education may be biased because the investment company has most to gain from you investing in the plan. To compound the problem, you are stuck with its biased advice because your company will not bring in an independent company (not responsible for the plan) to provide you unbiased education. Company human resources and legal personnel believe that if they attempt to help you, and your investments lose money, you may hold them responsible for those losses, and you will seek legal remedies against the company. Because financial advisors from an investment company are not compensated for educating you about investment choices and the true risk of your 401(k) allocations, they generally do not spend enough time teaching you what you need to know. Therefore, your responsibility is to arm yourself with unbiased financial knowledge, so that you can make better financial decisions and protect your financial future.

You need three things to adequately arm yourself: information, financial skills and motivation. Earlier chapters gave you the basic financial skills and motivation. This financial fitness step focuses on where you can get the information you need to build upon those skills and provides a sample schedule of activities you can use to guide your self-education.

Begin educating yourself by adjusting your listening, reading, and television viewing habits to incorporate more financial and investment information. You will want to spend a minimum of two to three hours per week on your financial education. This dedicated time (no distractions) can be at any time of the day or night, and can be increased as your capacity and motivation increase. Following is a sample schedule you can use as a guide to allocating time to your financial learning activities.

SAMPLE DAILY FINANCIAL LEARNING SCHEDULE

	Monday	Tuesday	Wednesday	Thursday	Friday	Saturday/Sunday
6 a.m.	Radio ▶					
7 a.m.	Newspaper ▶					
8 a.m.						Library
9 a.m.						
12 p.m.	Magazines ▶					
1 p.m.						
2 p.m.						
3 p.m.						
4 p.m.						
5 p.m.						Bookstore
6 p.m.	TV Programs ▶					
7 p.m.	TV Programs ▶					
8 p.m.						
9 p.m.						
10 p.m.	Books ▶					
11 p.m.	Books ▶					
12 a.m.	Internet ▶					

Maintaining a daily learning schedule is an easy way to increase your financial confidence. Be it early in the morning before work, over lunch, or in the evening, additional reading supplemented by a daily regimen of financial or investment programs on the radio or television will get you on the right track. It is also a good idea to encourage your family members to participate in daily financial learning activities. You can further supplement your education program by attending seminars, workshops and employer-sponsored classes.

If you follow a consistent but flexible schedule of financial education, you will increase your knowledge and will be more informed about making financial decisions. Both your confidence and your ability to reach your goals will be enhanced by the knowledge you will gain from your program. On July 10, 2003, the *USA Today Snapshot* reported that 85 percent of investors had the same or less confidence in their investing skills than they had the previous year. Every year, your confidence should increase from the daily educational program you outline for yourself.

Once you have your financial education schedule in place, you can review various information sources to determine which ones you will use to fill in the time slots. Pick the shows you will watch or listen to, and the books, magazines, and newspapers you will read.

Exhibit 5 lists a sampling of resources you can use to get financial information. There are many sources, old and new, so search the library, television, radio, bookstores, and the internet for financial information of interest. On the internet, you can use any search engine to type in such words as financial information, investing, financial education, retirement, credit and banking, insurance, taxes, and more, and you will discover a plethora of reference sources for these topics. You can also locate academic research papers and studies that shed light on the financial services industry, its problems and opportunities, and on human behavior and the psychology of investing. Locate and read as many of these as possible. These papers can have great research, information, and real-life examples that will be of value to you. In one such paper, Federal Reserve Chairman Alan Greenspan is quoted as saying, " Comprehensive education can help provide individuals with the financial knowledge necessary to create household budgets, initiate savings plans, manage debt, and make strategic investment decisions for their retirement."

Exhibit 5
Financial Resources

- *Wall Street Journal*
- *USA Today* (Money Section)
- *Investor's Business Daily*
- *Forbes*
- *Fortune*
- *The Great 401(k) Hoax,* by William Wolman and Anne Colamosca
- *Take on the Street: What Wall Street and Corporate America Don't Want You to Know,* by Arthur Levitt (with Paula Dwyer)
- *Moneyline* on CNN
- *Nightly Business Report on PBS*
- CBS.MarketWatch.com
- Quicken.com
- *Black Enterprise Magazine*
- *The Millionaire Mind,* by Thomas J. Stanley
- *Rich Dad, Poor Dad: What the Rich Teach Their Kids about Money—That the Poor and Middle Class Do Not!,* by Robert T. Kiyosaki
- DirectInvesting.com
- *Worry-Free Investing: A Safe Approach to Achieving Your Lifetime Financial Goals,* by Zvi Bodie and Michael J. Clowes
- *The 9 Steps to Financial Freedom,* by Suze Orman
- The Federal Reserve Chairman
- *Financial Fitness* (CD), by Tony Bland
- Mutual fund prospectuses

If you are just starting out, concentrate on the lighter, more entertaining financial shows, books, magazines, and newspapers. If you are more experienced in financial matters, challenge yourself to expand your knowledge outside your comfort zone. A research study by Maki (2001) argued that a greater knowledge of what is possible is the primary mechanism through which these (educational) programs alter household decision-making. In other words, the more knowledge you have, the greater likelihood you will make a better decision than you would make with less knowledge.

In addition to these information sources, you can pick the brain of a financial advisor who is a friend; a good, non-threatening way to learn more about money. It will be safe to ask "dumb" questions without feeling you're being judged or that you are the target of a sales pitch. Advisors who are friends will feel good that their friends (whom they respect) are asking for their expertise. You can also use the advisors as a sounding board for recommendations other people may give to you.

A recent survey of workers suggested that after completing a financial education program, individuals are likely to reevaluate their lifetime plans for work and retirement and savings and consumption (spending). So, keep on learning and make financial education a lifelong activity!

SPECIAL SECTION

FINANCIAL MAKEOVERS
- Need a Quick Fix -

For those on the verge of making a major financial decision and in need of a quick financial review (before working through *Six Steps to Financial Fitness*), let's take a look at two real-life financial makeovers (abbreviated) that you can use as a guide to quickly review and restructure your finances.

Makeover #1

Situation:
A young couple, twenty-five and twenty-seven years of age, married two years, purchased a home one year ago. The mortgage interest rate is 7 percent fixed for thirty years. Both husband and wife are employed, although they do not make enough money to sustain their current lifestyle. They keep track of their expenses monthly. They pay $140 per month in freeway tolls to get to and from their jobs. The husband has been offered the family business, which if taken, would allow them to earn more than enough money to meet their lifestyle needs. Prior to the home purchase, they saved $2,000 per month.

Before Makeover.........
Goal: Manage expenses and build up savings

1. Lifestyle = zero surplus
2. Emergency = zero
3. Accumulation = zero
4. Education = grad school plans
5. Retirement = $6,671
6. Legacy = no will

Immediate concerns:
- Improve cash flow/surplus
- Refinance or sell the new home
- Credit card balances at 17 percent
- Retirement planning

This couple should not sell their home. It is in a good neighborhood and will appreciate in value. Also, they should not refinance the mortgage. They have a good fixed rate and refinancing will only generate more costs and fees, adding to the total debt on the house. Rates are always moving up or down, so if you have a good one, don't second-guess it. Move on. The rule of thumb used to be: a 2-percent lower rate justifies a refinance. Now, an interest rate drop of 1 percent can be justification for refinance. In this couple's case, the rate would lower by a quarter point, and the payback for the cost of the refinance is over five years. Because they are not sure how long they will stay in the home, it's best for them to sit tight for now. A quarter percent over thirty years adds up to a significant amount of money, but over five years the money saved is insignificant. By bagging lunches and eliminating fast food dinners, the couple saves $660 per month. Consolidating credit cards at a lower rate saves $155 per month, and controlling clothes shopping saves an additional $250 per month. Because the wife has to spend for tuition upfront, it is a good idea for her to put off the grad school plans until cash flow is stabilized. As soon as the couple's cash flow provides, she should begin to contribute to her 401(k) plan to take advantage of her employer's matching contribution of 50 percent up to 4 percent of her salary. In the future, they should not live where tolls are a factor. The $140 per month they pay in tolls, over thirty years at an 8-percent return rate is approximately $152,000. That is money that could have been used to pay down the mortgage or for a retirement nest egg. Their retirement account choices should be moderate to conservative as they continue to grow in their knowledge of investing. This couple needs to bite the bullet on previous apartment-style living and buckle down in the real world of home ownership and responsibility.

Key Recommendations:

- Do not sell or refinance home
- Consolidate credit to lower rate
- Bag lunch and eat dinner at home

- Put off grad school
- Increase income
- Do not be afraid to fail
- In the future, do not purchase the freeway

After Makeover:

1. Lifestyle = Save $1,065 monthly
2. Emergency = Allocate from savings
3. Accumulation = Allocate from savings
4. Education = Hold off until cash flow is stable
5. Retirement = Get 401(k) plan employer match
6. Legacy = Get a will and insurance on husband

Makeover #2

Situation:
A couple, both in their forties, whose income has doubled over the past four years to $180,000. Both husband and wife are CPAs, and they have been married for six years. This is a classic example of a couple whose income has risen and they spend every last penny on trivial items.

Before Makeover ....
Goal: Reduce debt and purchase a new home in three years

1. Lifestyle = negative surplus
2. Emergency = zero
3. Accumulation = $4,500
4. Education = grad school plans and $13,000 pre-pay for children
5. Retirement = $100,000
6. Legacy = no will or life insurance on husband

Immediate concerns:

- New auto purchase
- Refinance home
- Grad school costs $40,000
- Retirement in 15 years with $250,000 to $500,000
- Tax refund of $3,000

This couple has a blended family of five children and needs to establish an estate plan for distribution of assets upon death. By not refinancing their house, they save $14,000 in debt and $400 monthly. Because they are planning to purchase a new home in three years, and refinancing to a 15-year mortgage will raise their monthly mortgage payment, cost thousands in fees and further drain their already negative cash flow, it does not make sense to refinance the mortgage. Eliminating the current graduate school plans and instead going to a school for which the employer will reimburse tuition saves $40,000 and $600 per month. By keeping the old current car, the couple saves $530 per month (and $31,800, the cost of her dream new car). Taking the unused education plan money ($13,000) the children chose not to use (the parents borrowed money to pay out-of-state tuition) and placing it in the accumulation fund gives the couple a head start on their new home. Their current $100,000 in retirement accounts can grow to $372,000 at 8 percent over their remaining pre-retirement years. By managing their newfound income, this couple can accelerate themselves into a potential early retirement. For now though, they need to extend their retirement age five years to ensure they achieve their retirement goals. Cutting back on the tens of thousands spent annually on clothing, other material purchases, and eating at expensive restaurants, will stop the depletion of their surplus cash and minimize credit card debt. This couple needs to decrease frivolous spending, and accelerate investments in their 401(k) plans. They need to reallocate their 401(k) investment choices to be more conservative than their current aggressive allocation, which has continued to result in big investment losses. They also need to put themselves on a consistent plan to increase their investment knowledge and review their investment statements, which they usually ignore most of the year. They need to get adequate life insurance on the husband.

Key recommendations:

- Do not refinance home
- Extend retirement to ages fifty-eight and sixty-two
- Spend below means
- Accumulate for new home
- Leave new car at the dealer
- Save future bonuses
- Get an estate plan

After Makeover:

1. Lifestyle = Save $85,800 in debt and $1,530 per month
2. Emergency = $4,500 stock sale and $1,500 tax refund
3. Accumulation = $1,500 tax refund and $13,000 education fund
4. Education = Change grad school plans
5. Retirement = $372,000 minimum
6. Legacy = Get an estate plan and life insurance on husband

Both these couples felt their spending was out of control and both were about to make major financial decisions. They needed a quick fix to stop the bleeding. The makeover is a short-term solution for quickly putting current financial issues in perspective and building the confidence to work through *Six Steps to Financial Fitness*. To make it work though, you have to open up your finances to constructive criticism and find either a single advisor or team of advisors knowledgeable in the areas of banking, credit, investments, insurance, and estate planning.

You now know *Six Steps to Financial Fitness*. These six steps are: (1) Set Goals and Strategies, (2) Create Cash Surplus, (3) Manage Cash Surplus and Pick Good Investments, (4) Pick Good Advisors, (5) Leave a Legacy, and (6) Increase Your Financial Knowledge. You have the information, financial skills, and motivation, along with a proven funding model for your cash surplus, to pick a good advisor and smart investments, construct a daily learning schedule, and to leave an appropriate legacy for your loved ones to enjoy. Now is the time to take control of your financial future. Start today to plan your financial future with confidence. Just write down your first lifestyle goal and you will be on your way to becoming financially fit!

APPENDIX

Estate Planning Documents

Estate Planning Questionnaire

Date:_____

A. General Information

1. Name.

    a. Full name:

    b. Names, other than the name set forth above, by which you have been or are now known:

2. Address.

    a. Present residence address: _____

    _____

    b. Residence address other than above address:
        (if none, skip to e.)

    _____

    _____

    c. Average length of time spent annually at each address: _____

    _____

    d. Address considered to be permanent address:

    _____

    _____

    e. Length of time resided in state of domicile:
        County of _____ : _____

    _____

APPENDIX 75

      f.   State or country of previous residence:
                _____

                _____

      g.   Do you intend to remain a permanent resident of your state of domicile?   Yes _____ No _____

3.   Telephone Numbers.

      a.   Residence: _____

      b.   Business: _____

               Fax: _____

4.   Social Security Number: _____

5.   Birth.

      a.   Date of Birth: _____

      b.   Place of Birth: _____
               (city, state or province, country)

      c.   Birth certificate: Yes_____ No_____
               (If yes, skip to 6).

      d.   If no, location of birth certificate: _____

               _____

6.   Citizenship.

      a.   Citizen of United States? Yes_____ No_____
               (If no, skip to d).

      b.   If citizen of United States: By birth _____
               (if by birth, skip to 7) naturalized ___.

      c.   If naturalized, specify:

(1) Place of naturalization (final papers):
_____

(2) Place of naturalization:
_____

(3) Naturalization certificate no.:
_____

(4) Location of naturalization certificate:
_____

d. If not citizen of United States, citizen of what country?
_____

e. Lawful permanent resident of United States (that is, green card holder)? Yes_____ No_____.

f. Alien Certificate of Registration No.
_____

7. Financial Advisors.

List the names and addresses of your financial advisors including but not limited to your accountant, life insurance agent, investment advisor, and other attorneys.

_____

_____

_____

_____

_____

_____

B. Family Information

1. Current Marital Status.

    a. Married: _____.

    b. Divorced or marriage dissolved, or annulled: _____.

    c. Separated: _____.

    d. Widowed: _____.

    e. Never married: _____.

2. If Married: (if not married, skip to 3)

    a. Name of spouse:

    b. Other names used by spouse:

    c. Date of spouse's birth:

    d. Place of spouse's birth:

    e. Spouse's Social Security number:

    i. Citizenship of spouse:

j.   Address of spouse (if different from 2.a):
_____
_____

k.   Telephone numbers of spouse:

Residence: _____

Business: _____

l.   Spouse's occupation or profession:
_____

m.   Spouse's employer:
_____

n.   Spouse's employer's address:
_____
_____

o.   Spouse previously married? Yes_____ No_____

p.   If spouse was previously married, how was marriage terminated?
_____

   (1) If marriage was terminated by divorce, dissolution of marriage, or annulment, specify details, including:

      1) Name of prior spouse:
      _____

      2) Date and place of prior marriage:
      _____

      3) Date of termination of prior marriage:

APPENDIX 79

_____

4) Court that terminated prior marriage:
_____

Case number _____

5) Property settlement agreement: (specify details) _____
_____
_____
_____

(2) If prior marriage was terminated by death, specify:

1) Date of death: _____

2) Place of death: _____

q. Are you party to any antenuptial agreement:
Yes _____ No _____.

(1) Location of agreement:
_____

(2) General contents of agreement:
_____
_____

3. If you are divorced or prior marriage was terminated by dissolution or annulment:

    a. Name of prior spouse:
_____

b.   Date and place of prior marriage:
    _____

c.   Name of state and court in which decree of divorce, dissolution, or annulment was entered:
    _____

d.   Date of decree:
    _____

e.   General contents of decree with respect to support and property rights:
    _____
    _____
    _____

f.   General contents of any property settlement agreement or alimony or support agreement or trust:
    _____
    _____
    _____
    _____

4. If Separated:

    a.   Name of spouse:
        _____

    b.   Address:
        _____
        _____

    c.   Date and place of marriage:
        _____

    d.   Name of state and court in which separation decree

was entered:
_____

e. Date of decree:
_____

f. General contents of decree with respect to support and property rights:
_____
_____
_____

g. General contents of any separation agreement with respect to support and property rights:
_____
_____
_____
_____

5. If Widowed:

a. Name of spouse:
_____

b. Date of marriage:
_____

c. Date of spouse's death:
_____

d. Place of spouse's death:
_____

e. Spouse died: testate _____ intestate _____

f. Has spouse's estate been administered?
Yes _____ No _____

g. Name of state and court in which spouse's estate was or is being administered: _____

Case No._____

h. If estate is still being administered, general status of administration: _____

_____

i. Your interest (as heir, legatee, devisee, creditor, etc.) in spouse's estate: _____

_____

6. Next of Kin.

(Include children born out of wedlock, adopted children, and children of deceased children.)

Name: _____

Address: _____

_____

Date of Birth: _____

Relationship: _____

Social Security No.: _____

Name: _____

Address: _____

_____

Date of Birth: _____

Relationship: _____

Social Security No.: _____

Name: _____

Address: _____

_____

Date of Birth: _____

Relationship: _____

Social Security No.: _____

Name: _____

Address: _____

_____

Date of Birth: _____

Relationship: _____

Social Security No.: _____

C. Military Service

1. United States Military Service? Yes _____ No _____
2. Military Service in Foreign Countries: Yes _____ No _____

a. Country: _____

b. If Discharged, Location of Discharge Papers:
_____

D. Employment and Employment Benefits

1. If Employed (including employment by closely-held corporation):

   a. Name of employer:
   _____

   b. Address:
   _____
   _____

   c. Telephone number: _____

   d. Date employed: _____

   e. General contents of employment agreement, if any:
   _____
   _____
   _____
   _____

   f. Employment benefits (specify company, amount, beneficiary, as appropriate).

      (1) Health and accident insurance:
      _____

      (2) Life insurance:
      _____

      (3) Pension:

(4) Profit sharing: _____

(5) Stock options: _____

(6) Other benefits: _____

2. If Self-Employed:

    a. Name of business: _____

    b. Address: _____

    c. Telephone Number: _____

    d. Nature of business: _____

    e. Have you established self-employment pension plan: Yes _____ No _____

    f. If yes, general contents of plan: _____

3. If Retired:

    a. Date of retirement: _____

b. Type of pension plan and balance in plan:

(1) Defined benefit plan
___

(2) Target benefit plan
___

(3) Defined contribution plan
___

(4) Money-purchase plan
___

(5) Trusteed plan
___

(6) Custodial plan
___

(7) Annuity plan
___

(8) Face-amount certificate plan
___

(9) Government retirement bond plan
___

(10) Employee contributory plan
___

(11) Employee noncontributory plan
___

(12) IRA plan
___

(13) Keogh plan
___

(14)   Military pension plan and bonuses
_____

(15)   United States Civil Service Retirement pension plan
_____

(16)   Railroad retirement pension plan
_____

(17)   State or local government pension plan
_____

(18)   Other type of plan: (specify)
_____

c.   Details of plan: _____
_____

E. Safe Deposit Boxes

1.   Box Number   Bank or trust company where located and branch

  1)_____ _____

  2)_____ _____

  3)_____ _____

  4)_____ _____

  5)_____ _____

2.   For each box number listed above, specify the following:

  a.   Name in which box is held:

      1) _____

2) _____

3) _____

4) _____

5) _____

    b.   Persons entitled to enter box:

1) _____

2) _____

3) _____

4) _____

5) _____

F. Bank and Credit Union Accounts

1.

Account No.	Bank	Address	Amount

1) _____ _____

2) _____ _____

3) _____ _____

4) _____ _____

5) _____ _____

2. For each account listed above, please specify:

    a. Type of account;

        1) _____

        2) _____

        3) _____

        4) _____

        5) _____

    b. How account is titled:

        1) _____

        2) _____

        3) _____

        4) _____

G. Insurance

1. Life Insurance:

      1) Company_____

      Policy No. _____Face Amount: _____

      Insured _____

      Owner _____

      Beneficiary _____

      2) Company_____

Policy No. _____ Face Amount: _____

Insured _____

Owner _____

Beneficiary _____

3) Company_____

Policy No. _____ Face Amount: _____

Insured _____

Owner _____

Beneficiary _____

4) Company_____

Policy No. _____ Face Amount: _____

Insured _____

Owner _____

Beneficiary _____

5) Company_____

Policy No. _____ Face Amount: _____

Insured _____

Owner _____

Beneficiary _____

2. Other Insurance:

    1) Company _____

        Policy No._____

        Kind & Amount_____

    2) Company _____

        Policy No._____

        Kind & Amount_____

    3) Company _____

        Policy No._____

        Kind & Amount_____

    4) Company _____

        Policy No._____

        Kind & Amount_____

    5) Company _____

        Policy No._____

        Kind & Amount_____

H. Real Property

1.   <u>Location</u>   <u>Description</u>

   1) _____ _____

   2) _____ _____

   3) _____ _____

   4) _____ _____

   5) _____ _____

2. For real property listed above, please specify:

   a. How title is held:

      1) _____

      2) _____

      3) _____

      4) _____

      5) _____

   b. Purchase price/present value (gross, before any mortgages):

      1) _____ / _____

      2) _____ / _____

      3) _____ / _____

      4) _____ / _____

      5) _____ / _____

c. Date of purchase:

1) _____

2) _____

3) _____

4) _____

5) _____

d. Amount of mortgage or other lien:

1) _____

2) _____

3) _____

4) _____

5) _____

I. Personal Property

1. Furniture and Furnishings; Household Goods and Appliances: (unique or valuable)

<u>Article and Description</u>   <u>Value</u>

a._____ _____

b._____ _____

c._____ _____

d._____ _____

e._____ _____

2. Motor Vehicles; Boats; Aircraft:

<u>Make and Model</u>   <u>Title Holder</u>   <u>Year</u>   <u>Value</u>

a._____ _____ _____ _____

b._____ _____ _____ _____

c._____ _____ _____ _____

d._____ _____ _____ _____

e._____ _____ _____ _____

3. Stamp and Coin Collections; Paintings and Other Art Objects:

<u>Description</u>   <u>Value</u>   <u>Location</u>

a._____ _____ _____

b._____ _____ _____

c._____ _____ _____

d._____ _____ _____

e._____ _____ _____

J. Securities or Brokerage Accounts

1. <u>Name and type of security (attach statement, if easier)</u>   <u>Value</u>

a._____ _____ _____

b._____ _____ _____

c._____ _____ _____

d._____ _____ _____

e._____ _____ _____

K. Business Interests

<u>VALUE</u>

1. a._____ _____

   b._____ _____

   c._____ _____

   d._____ _____

   e._____ _____

2. For each business listed above, please specify the following:

   <u>Form of Organization</u>   <u>Ownership</u>

   a._____ _____

   b._____ _____

   c._____ _____

   d._____ _____

   e._____ _____

L. Patents, Copyrights, Franchises, etc.

	Type	Name of Interest	Date of Acquisition	Value
1.	_____	_____	_____	_____
2.	_____	_____	_____	_____
3.	_____	_____	_____	_____
4.	_____	_____	_____	_____
5.	_____	_____	_____	_____

M. Obligations Owed

Description of Debt	Evidence of Debt
a. _____	_____
b. _____	_____
c. _____	_____
d. _____	_____
e. _____	_____

1. For each debt listed above, please specify:

Balance Due	Name of Debtor
a. _____	_____
b. _____	_____
c. _____	_____

d._____ _____

e._____ _____

N. Interest in Trusts and Estates

1. Are you a trustee or beneficiary of any Trust?
   Yes _____ No _____

   General contents of trust instrument:
   _____
   _____
   _____
   _____

2. Do you expect inheritance from persons other than deceased spouse? Yes _____ No _____

   a. Estate(s) of _____

   b. General analysis of status and rights:
   _____
   _____
   _____
   _____

O. Obligations Owed
(other than those listed in H, above)

1.   <u>Nature of Obligation</u>   <u>Evidence of Obligation</u>

   a. _____ _____

   b. _____ _____

   c. _____ _____

2. For each obligation listed above, please specify:

   <u>Name of Creditor</u>   <u>Amount of Obligation</u>

   a. _____ _____

   b. _____ _____

   c. _____ _____

P. Pending Litigation

1.   <u>Nature of Dispute</u>   <u>Amount in Controversy</u>

   a. _____ _____

   b. _____ _____

   c. _____ _____

2. For each case listed above, specify:

   a.   Are you plaintiff or defendant?

       1) _____

2) _____

3) _____

    b.   Current status of litigation:

1) _____

2) _____

3) _____

    c.   Name and address of attorney representing you:

1) _____

2) _____

3) _____

Q. Inter Vivos Trusts Established or to Be Established by You

1.   *Existing Trusts:*

    A. <u>Beneficiaries of Existing Trusts</u> <u>Date Established</u> <u>Value</u>

1._____ _____ _____

2._____ _____ _____

3._____ _____ _____

    B.   For each trust listed above, specify:

1. Is trust revocable or irrevocable?

a) _____

b) _____

c) _____

2. Name of trustee:

a) _____

b) _____

c) _____

2. *Trusts to be Established:*

A. <u>Beneficiaries</u> <u>Percentage or Amount to Receive</u>

1) _____

2) _____

3) _____

B. Names of Trustees and Order of Appointment:

1) _____

2) _____

3) _____

C. Age at which children may serve as trustees of their own trusts: _____

R. Gifts

1. **Type of Gift**   **Donee**   **Value**

   a. _____ _____ _____

   b. _____ _____ _____

   c. _____ _____ _____

2. Gift tax returns filed? Yes _____ No _____

3. If filed, prepared by:

   Name: _____

   Address: _____

S. Personal Representative

List the names and addresses of the persons you would appoint to administer your estate. Individuals must be related or residents of state of domicile. (It is a good idea to name several people in this regard, with an indication of the order of preference. If married and you appoint your spouse, indicate "reciprocal" if he/she appoints you to serve in such capacity as well.).

_____

_____

_____

_____

T. Guardians of Minor Children

List names and addresses of persons you would appoint to serve as guardians of the person and property of any child of yours who is under the age of majority in the event both you and your spouse are either deceased or unable to care for such child. (It is a good idea to name several people in this regard, with an indication of the order of preference.)

_____

_____

_____

_____

If the proposed guardians are a married couple, would you want them to serve together initially, with one serving alone if the other becomes unable or unwilling? Yes _____; No _____.

U. Health Care Surrogate/Preneed Guardian

1. List the name(s) and address(es), in order of preference if more than one, of persons you would appoint to act as your health care surrogate if you are unable to communicate your wishes relative to your care and treatment. (If married and you appoint your spouse, indicate "reciprocal" if he/she appoints you to serve in such capacity, as well.)

    _____

    _____

    _____

    _____

2. List the name(s) and address(es), in order of preference if more than one, of persons you would appoint to act as your Guardian if you are adjudged incompetent. (If married and you

appoint your spouse, indicate "reciprocal" if he/she appoints you to serve in such capacity, as well.)

_____

_____

_____

_____

V. Attorney-in-Fact

List the name(s) and address(es), in order of preference if more than one, of persons you would appoint to serve as your Attorney-in-Fact (through the granting of a Durable General Power of Attorney) to perform certain specified tasks in your absence or inability to perform them yourself. (If married and you appoint your spouse, indicate "reciprocal" if he/she appoints you to serve in such capacity, as well.)

_____

_____

_____

_____

Documents

The documents listed below are all important to the development of your estate plan. Because these documents contain technical legal details that should be analyzed by a lawyer it is important that you furnish a copy of each, if at all possible.

1. Present your Will and your spouse's Will

2. The trust instrument for any trust created by you or your spouse

3. The trust instrument of any trust under which you, your spouse, or any of your children are a beneficiary or have any other interests

4. Gift tax returns (all)

5. Stockholder or partnership agreements (including buy-sell agreements)

6. Instruments under which you or your spouse have a power of appointment

7. Prenuptial or postnuptial agreements or separation agreements

8. Powers of attorney held or authorized by you or your spouse

If a revocable funded living trust is being established for you, the following additional documents will be required:

1. Deeds for all real property

2. Retirement plan statements and agreements

3. Life insurance policies

4. List of tangible personal property

5. Bank statements

6. Brokerage account statements

7. Bonds/Stocks

8. Corporate Books

9. Partnership agreements

10. Notes receivable

Estate Planning Checklist

1. Is there a Last Will and Testament?

2. Are Revocable Living Trusts being used to avoid probate and guardianship? Have such trusts been properly funded?

3. Has family established financial powers of attorney for management of assets in situations of incapacity?

4. Is there a Health Care Surrogate and Living Will in place for situations of incapacity?

5. Is there a guardian appointed to become the surrogate parent of any minor children?

6. Is there an alternate custodian on Gift to Minors Act accounts? If donor to the account is a custodian, the account will be subject to estate tax on donor's death.

7. Is the proper party named trustee for the assets of the children? Is the most trusted relative better suited to serve as a co-trustee with a trust company or a professional advisor? Is a guardian who also serves as a trustee better suited to serve as a co-trustee so that there are checks and balances?

8. With regard to leaving property in trust for children, do such trusts release at certain ages or continue for the lifetime of the child to provide protection from divorce, creditor claims and estate tax in the child's estate (i.e., generation skip)?

9. Does the estate plan provide for a by-pass trust to utilize the applicable credit amount (currently $1.5 million) that could benefit the surviving spouse without being subject to estate tax on the second death? Have assets or beneficiary designations been properly coordinated to fund such trust without triggering

income tax on the first death?

10. Does the estate plan take advantage of the generation skipping-exemption (currently $1.12 million)

11. Does the estate plan provide for marital deduction trusts for amounts above the applicable credit to creditor and divorce protect the surviving spouse?

12. Are the lawyer, accountant, insurance professional, financial planner, trust company and other involved professionals aware of the plan's basic logistics?

13. Is the plan reviewed periodically?

EPILOGUE

For those who know me best, this book is no surprise. The vision for *Six Steps to Financial Fitness* comes directly from God and is a result of my calling to educate you, the consumer, about ways to improve your financial life.

I am truly blessed with the opportunity to communicate to you my perspective and *Six Steps to Financial Fitness*. These six steps—(1) Set Goals and Strategies, (2) Create Cash Surplus, (3) Manage Cash Surplus and Pick Good Investments, (4) Pick Good Advisors, (5) Leave a Legacy, and (6) Increase Your Financial Knowledge—are the foundation for creating and fulfilling your financial destiny.

While writing *Six Steps to Financial Fitness*, I was encouraged by my personal clients and all of you who attended my workshops and seminars around the country. You are so eager to learn ways to gain control of your finances, make better investments, and understand the true risks of your 401(k)s. Please continue your curiosity about financial products and strategies. Your curiosity is a stimulus to becoming financially fit.

Finally, it has been confirmed to me throughout this process that financial strategies are much more important than financial products. But, to develop good strategies, you must be aware of the products that are available to you, their characteristics, their pros and cons. You must also beware of the financial advisor who encourages you to take risk when you are not comfortable with that risk, whether it is with mutual funds, variable life insurance, or with variable-rate mortgages. So, don't be afraid to be conservative, regardless your age or circumstances.

I've learned that you can become your own best advocate by increasing your financial knowledge, establishing your financial lifestyle, and going with your gut when it comes to making financial decisions. When you make "gut" decisions you are instinctively balancing your risk tolerance with your knowledge of financial products. So, work with a plan, learn as much as you can, trust your instincts, don't lose money, and you'll say what my friend Ernestine says after making her quarterly financial decisions, "Now, I can sleep better at night."

Further Reading

Financial terminology can be confusing and sometimes misleading. To provide you with a source for finding information on financial products and learning financial terminology, I recommend you purchase two books.

Barron's *Finance and Investment Handbook,* Sixth Edition, by John Downes and Jordan Elliot Goodman is a great information source when you need facts, figures, names, addresses, and telephone numbers in the finance and investment world.

Barron's Guide to Making Investment Decisions by Douglas Sease and John A. Prestbo is a guide to understand product definitions and investment strategies for use with your personal investment portfolio.

Both books are very readable and along with *Six Steps to Financial Fitness* should be made the cornerstone of your financial library.

Good luck and good reading.

Infinite Possibilities Publishing Group, Inc.
P.O. Box 150823
Altamonte Springs, FL 32715-0823
Office: (407) 699-6603
Fax: (407) 331-3926

ORDER FORM

For Office Use Only
| ON# |
| OD |
| SD |
| AUTH# |
| BY: |

Bill to:

Name _____

Business Name _____

Street Address (no P.O. Boxes) _____ / _____ Apt./Suite

City _____ State _____ Zip _____

Daytime Phone _____

e-mail Address: _____

Ship to:

Name _____

Business Name _____

Street Address (no P.O. Boxes) _____ / _____ Apt./Suite

City _____ State _____ Zip _____

Daytime Phone _____

Qty	Item#	Title/Description	Item Price	Total
	09-1263-5	Six Steps To Financial Fitness by Tony Bland	13.95	

PAYMENT METHOD:
☐ Visa®   ☐ Master Card®
☐ American Express®   ☐ Discover®

___/___/___/___/___/___/___/___/___/___/___/___/
Card Number

___/___
Exp. Date   Signature *(required for credit card payment)*

☐ Check for total amount enclosed

Sub-total	
Shipping & Handling*	4.95
Sales Tax: (FL Residents Apply 7%)	
GRAND TOTAL	

Fax Completed Form to: (407) 331-3926

or Mail Completed Form to:
IP Publishing Group, Inc.
P.O. Box 150823
Altamonte Springs, FL 32715-0823

NOTE
Returned checks subject to a service charge of $25 or the maximum allowed by law.
All non-Florida residents: you are responsible for the use tax
(if applicable in the state in which the book is shipped)

*For orders of 3 or more, please call (407) 699-6603 for shipping costs.

Thank you for your order!